Original title:
Winter's Solitude

Copyright © 2024 Swan Charm
All rights reserved.

Author: Linda Leevike
ISBN HARDBACK: 978-9908-52-128-2
ISBN PAPERBACK: 978-9908-52-129-9
ISBN EBOOK: 978-9908-52-130-5

Melancholy in the Crystal Silence

In the stillness of the night,
A whisper floats like ghostly light.
Shadows dance on walls so bare,
Echoes linger in the air.

Moonlight paints a world so pale,
Each heartbeat tells a secret tale.
Lingering thoughts stretch like a thread,
A solitude, where dreams are fed.

Hushed are voices, lost in time,
Words unspoken, lost in rhyme.
Frozen laughter drifts away,
As night swallows the fading day.

Beneath the stars, a sighing wind,
Reveals the pain of what has sinned.
Tears are shed in silence deep,
A love once cherished, now to keep.

Fading visions intertwine,
In shadows where the memories shine.
Melancholy sings its tune,
Beneath the watchful, waning moon.

The Frozen Beauty of Distant Memory

In a whispering, snow-clad vale,
Time stands still, as dreams exhale.
Each flake dances like a thought,
Frigid echoes, love once sought.

Faces shimmer, lost in haze,
Reflections caught in winter's gaze.
Branches bend with crystal weight,
Moments frozen, sealed by fate.

Hazy dawn, a soft embrace,
Illuminates a timeless place.
Heartbeats trace a gentle line,
Through the frost, our souls entwine.

Whispers of a faded song,
Call to minds where we belong.
Scattered dreams like twinkling stars,
Glimmer brightly, though they're far.

In this quiet, frozen sphere,
Beauty lingers, ever near.
Distant echoes call us home,
In memory's embrace, we roam.

Serenity Amidst a Frigid Silence

An untouched world of purest white,
Blankets quiet under night.
Gentle stillness wraps the ground,
In this peace, no fear is found.

Snowflakes whisper, secrets shared,
Nature rests, her heart laid bare.
Softly glistening, the moonbeam's glow,
Guides the path where kindred flow.

A fleeting breath on frosty air,
Moments taken, lives laid bare.
Within the chill, a warmth does rise,
In the heart where true love lies.

Beneath the stars, hope takes flight,
Casting dreams into the night.
Serenity brims in every space,
Finding solace, grace, and grace.

In the embrace of frigid peace,
The tumult within begins to cease.
Together, we will find our way,
In silent beauty's soft array.

Murmurs of Nature's Stillness

In the hush of dawn's embrace,
A gentle sigh, a soft trace.
Leaves rustle with a muted sound,
In stillness, peace and calm are found.

Ripples dance on a glassy stream,
Nature sways in a quiet dream.
Birds whisper secrets through the trees,
As shadows flicker with the breeze.

Mountains stand in quiet might,
Guardians of the fading light.
The world breathes slow, a sacred rite,
In murmurs shared with fading night.

Moonlight spills on tranquil lakes,
Soft reflections, the heart awakes.
Stars adorn the velvet skies,
In this stillness, my soul flies.

Nature's song in every breath,
Whispers of life, hints of death.
Through the silence, wisdom flows,
In every pause, true beauty grows.

Breath of the Icy Air

Chill winds sweep through barren trees,
Whispers of winter, a biting freeze.
Icy tendrils cling to the ground,
In the quiet, dreams are found.

Snowflakes drift from clouds so gray,
Dancing softly, they lose their way.
Each flake a story, unique and bright,
In the stillness of the night.

Breath of cold, crisp and clear,
Frosted whispers, all that we hear.
A world transformed, a brilliant white,
In the heart of winter's light.

The frozen streams, a mirror's gaze,
Reflect the sun's soft golden rays.
Nature sleeps, but in repose,
Her beauty blooms, like winter's rose.

Beneath the ice, life still flows,
Hidden warmth where the heart knows.
In every breath, this chill we share,
Life resumes with the icy air.

Frosted Dreams of a Vanished Autumn

Leaves that danced in hues of gold,
Now lie silent, stories told.
Frosted edges, a crisp embrace,
Nature holds her gentle grace.

The sun dips low, the skies turn gray,
As autumn whispers soft goodbye.
Dreams of warmth in the fading light,
Nestle close as day turns night.

Vivid memories of bright decay,
A fleeting beauty fades away.
In every branch, a tale to weave,
Of warmth, of loss, and hearts that grieve.

Pine cones drop in the winter's chill,
Echoes linger, the quiet fills.
Frosty breath on a longing heart,
From autumn's end, we won't depart.

Hope resides in the frosted dreams,
As nature whispers her silent schemes.
With each change, the past we hold,
Envelops us in tales retold.

Serenity in the Whispering Winds

Winds caress the fields of green,
In gentle sweeps, the earth is seen.
Nature speaks in tones so pure,
In silent moments, we're assured.

Whispers float on evening air,
Carried softly, everywhere.
The world slows down, a breath taken,
In this stillness, hearts awaken.

Clouds drift lazily, shadows play,
Moments linger, gently sway.
A symphony of rustling trees,
Nature's balm brings us to ease.

As twilight falls, stars ignite,
In the darkness, beams of light.
The whispers of the winds unite,
With our spirits, take to flight.

In the calm, we find our truth,
The whispering winds speak our youth.
Through every breath of evening's song,
In serenity, we all belong.

The Quietude of the Frosted Night

Stars twinkle softly in the hush,
The moon casts silver on the snow,
Trees stand still, wrapped in calm,
A serene world under ice's glow.

Breath of winter, crisp and clear,
Whispers of time quietly unfold,
Each flake a gem, delicate sphere,
In this stillness, stories told.

Night wraps the earth in a cloak,
Every sound seems far away,
The heart speaks loud, yet remains broke,
In the beauty of this frozen play.

Deep in shadows, secrets kept,
Guarded by the chill of night,
Here in peace, no tears are wept,
Just the breath of stars, so bright.

Silent moments breathe relief,
Amidst the frost, we find our rest,
In quietude, we ease our grief,
Under the frost, we're truly blessed.

Echoing Footsteps on Frozen Ground

Echoes linger in the air,
Footsteps crackle on the ice,
Each step a tale, fraught with care,
Tracing paths, a silent vice.

Moonlight dances on the trail,
Shadows lengthen, stretch and yawn,
What lies beyond the frosty veil?
A world transformed at break of dawn.

Whispers of a winter's breath,
Curling fog, soft and slight,
Each footfall strips the world of death,
Eager hearts, ignited light.

Nature holds its breath and waits,
As the night wears on and on,
Frigid winds debate our fates,
Cradled softly, till the dawn.

In the silence, souls unite,
Paths converge on frozen ground,
In the stillness of the night,
Hope and warmth in whispers found.

Enigmatic Silence Beneath a Tattered Sky

Clouds hang low, a tattered shroud,
Thick with secrets, dark and deep,
Beneath the weight, silence is loud,
Starlight glimmers, a watchful sweep.

Whispers curl like smoke in air,
Hints of dreams lost along the way,
Each moment hangs, fragile and rare,
In shadows where the lost souls play.

A flicker of light, a ghostly sheen,
Nature breathes in solemn grace,
Lost in thoughts that once had been,
Each memory finds a sacred space.

The world stands still, time suspends,
In the quiet, shadows lie,
Wounds of the heart, the mind defends,
Beneath this endless, tattered sky.

In the silence, wisdom wakes,
Yearning echoes through the night,
In each breath, the world remakes,
Finding solace in the light.

Crystalline Whispers of the Night

Frosted landscapes glimmer bright,
Crystalline whispers fill the air,
Each breath a cloud, soft and light,
Nature's secrets, stark and rare.

Stars weave tales in glinting hues,
Painting stories on the dark,
Underneath this canvas, clues,
Of dreams ignited, a quiet spark.

Night unfolds like silken cloth,
Every corner wraps in grace,
In its grasp, we feel both swath
Of warmth and cold, a tender face.

Softly now, the world exhales,
Muffled thoughts drift through the peace,
In these whispers, magic trails,
Moments linger, worries cease.

Crystalline dreams take gentle flight,
Guided by the moon's embrace,
In the quiet of the night,
Our hearts find rest in this still space.

Silent Whispers of Frost

In the quiet of the night,
Frost lays a gentle kiss.
Whispers of the cold winds,
Speak of winter's bliss.

Silvery branches sway,
Underneath a starry dome.
Nature holds its breath tight,
As frost calls it home.

Footprints left in snow,
Lead to places unknown.
Echoes of laughter fade,
In the chill, all alone.

The moon glows brightly here,
Casting shadows so deep.
Secrets held in the night,
Where the cold promises keep.

In this frozen expanse,
Time seems to pause and wait.
Silent whispers of frost,
In a world wrapped in fate.

Embrace of the Snowbound

Wrapped in blankets of white,
Huddled in warmth's tender care.
Outside the snowflakes dance,
In the crisp, frosty air.

Each flake unique in form,
Drifting soft to the ground.
Nature's quilted embrace,
In silence all around.

The world feels soft and still,
Underneath this cold glow.
Whispers of winter's heart,
In each gentle flurry's flow.

Embrace of the snowbound,
Holds stories yet to be told.
Of warmth shared in shadows,
With memories brave and bold.

Through the chill, we find light,
In laughter, joy takes flight.
Together we stay warm,
In the snow's quiet night.

Veil of the Frosted Moon

Upon the midnight sky,
The frosted moon does gleam.
Veils of silver mist swirl,
Casting a haunting dream.

Stars twinkle far above,
In the stillness, they dance.
Under the moon's watchful eye,
The world holds its trance.

Frost bites at my cheeks,
As I wander through the night.
Every shadow tells tales,
In the soft, pale light.

The trees, a silent army,
Stand guard in frozen grace.
Veil of the frosted moon,
Hides secrets of this place.

In the quiet, time pauses,
Wrapped in the winter's spell.
Under the frost's embrace,
In the moonlight, we dwell.

Echoes in the Frozen Air

Whispers of the cold wind,
Carry tales of the night.
Echoes in the frozen air,
Dance in soft moonlight.

Each breath forms a cloud,
In the stillness, I stand.
Lost in thoughts of old times,
Tracing dreams in the sand.

The world around is hushed,
Each sound a fragile thread.
Echoes weave through the night,
In the silence, we're led.

Snowflakes drift and descend,
Painting the ground anew.
Whispers in the frozen air,
Share the stories of you.

As dawn begins to rise,
The echoes fade away.
In the heart of winter still,
Memories choose to stay.

Tranquil Stillness: A Frozen Heart

In silence falls the winter's breath,
A hush that speaks of quiet death.
The world wrapped tight in icy chains,
In frozen hearts, the stillness reigns.

Each flake a whisper, soft and white,
A dance of dreams in the pale light.
With every step, the world stands still,
In tranquil night, the heart doth chill.

Snow blankets hopes, so pure, so deep,
While shadows of the past still creep.
Yet in this quiet, there's a spark,
A hint of warmth to thaw the dark.

Paths Quieted by the Cold

Through the woods where shadows play,
The paths are quiet, lost in gray.
A soft embrace of winter's hand,
Guides each footfall through the land.

The crunch of snow beneath the feet,
A melody both calm and sweet.
In frosty air, the breath is seen,
Each moment cherished, pure, serene.

Leaves long gone, the branches bare,
A world transformed, beyond compare.
In the stillness of the chill,
Echoes linger, time stands still.

Distant Hearths and Hushed Woods

Beyond the hills, the hearths lie still,
Fires flicker, dreams they fill.
While woods around in silence sweep,
The secrets of the night they keep.

Stars above, a distant guide,
Through whispering pines, the shadows slide.
Each breath of wind a gentle sigh,
Where lingering thoughts and memories fly.

The moonlight spills on frosted ground,
In this stillness, peace is found.
Yet distant hearts begin to yearn,
For warmth and light, for love's return.

Solitary Pines, Frost Adorned

In solitary stands the pine,
Adorned in frost, a sight divine.
Each needle glints with icy grace,
A sentinel in this vast space.

Around it swirls the winter's kiss,
A tranquil world, a frosty bliss.
With roots that delve through snow and ice,
It holds the secrets, calm and nice.

Each day it braves the bitter cold,
A story waiting to be told.
In untouched snow, it finds its voice,
A poet's heart, a whispered choice.

Shadows Across the White Expanse

Shadows dance on snow so bright,
Whispers echo in the night.
Footprints lead where none remain,
Silent paths of joy and pain.

Moonlight casts a silver trace,
Haunting features of the place.
Every step a story told,
Nature's grip, both fierce and bold.

Chill of winter wraps the ground,
Beauty lost is seldom found.
Yet amid the frozen glow,
Hope persists where dreamers go.

Branches bow with crystal weight,
Lonely winds begin to wait.
In the stillness, secrets lie,
Beneath the vast, unyielding sky.

Yearning hearts find solace here,
In the cold, the warmth is near.
Shadows keep their gentle song,
Guiding souls where they belong.

Silence Among Frosty Pines

In the woods, a quiet plea,
Frosty pines stand tall and free.
Snowflakes fall without a sound,
Nature's peace, profound, unbound.

Beneath the boughs, the world feels still,
Whispers hush as spirits fill.
Every breath a frozen sigh,
Thoughts drift gently, like the sky.

Branches wear a snowy crown,
Winter wraps the earth like gown.
In this hidden sanctuary,
Close your eyes and simply be.

Echoes linger in the breeze,
Carried softly through the trees.
In the calm, the heart can sway,
Finding peace where shadows play.

Time feels paused, a perfect frame,
Nature's canvas, wild, untamed.
Among the pines, dreams intertwine,
Life unfolds, tender and divine.

Clouded Dreams in Crystal Form

Glimmers shine in misty light,
Clouded dreams take graceful flight.
Figures dance in fragile air,
Whispers haunt with gentle care.

Each breath forms a shadowed mist,
Silent echoes, softly kissed.
Through the haze, we reach for more,
Yearning for what's yet in store.

In the distance, visions fade,
Moments lost, yet love remains.
Crystals fall like tears from stars,
Marking where the journey starts.

Veils of fog conceal the truth,
Innocence of fleeting youth.
Clouds embrace the dreams we hold,
Stories wrapped in threads of gold.

As the daylight starts to break,
Hope awakens, hearts awake.
Through the clouds, our dreams transform,
In the light, we find our form.

Frosty Imprints of Time

Footprints traced in icy ground,
Whispers of what once was found.
Frosty imprints, memories clear,
Linking moments held so dear.

Gentle winds will carry tales,
Of laughter shared, of love that sails.
In the stillness, voices blend,
Echoes of the hearts we send.

Through the seasons, shapes will change,
Time moves on, but feels so strange.
Yet in the chill, our souls remain,
Bound by joy, by love, by pain.

Frost upon the windowpane,
Nature's art, a sweet refrain.
Glistening like memories bright,
Illumined by the silver light.

In each step, we leave a trace,
Marking time in this vast space.
Frosty imprints, our design,
Memories shared, forever shine.

The Quietude of Wistful Hours

In the fading light of day,
Memories come out to play.
Whispers of a time gone by,
In the stillness, dreams can lie.

The trees sway gently in the breeze,
Nature hums a soft reprise.
Stars emerge with silent grace,
Each one holds a secret place.

As the world begins to fade,
Hopes and wishes unafraid.
A quiet moment, hearts entwined,
In this hour, peace we find.

Time feels endless, yet so brief,
In the twilight, lies belief.
Holding on to what we know,
In the quiet, love can grow.

So let us savor every second,
In the stillness, we are beckoned.
With each breath, a promise new,
In the shadows, light shines through.

Frostbitten Poems in the Dark

Underneath the icy stars,
Silent dreams of distant bars.
Whispers travel through the night,
Frostbitten tales, whispered bright.

Moonlight dances on the frost,
In this darkness, we are lost.
Each breath mingles with the chill,
Every heartbeat, time stands still.

In the shadows, secrets seethe,
With the night, we dare believe.
Words emerge like flurries, free,
Poems penned in quiet glee.

The world outside is still and calm,
In this night, we find our balm.
Frostbitten verses, pure and stark,
Glowing softly in the dark.

So gather close, let stories flow,
In the winter's grasp, we know.
With every line, warmth ignites,
Frostbitten poems, shining lights.

Solitary Footprints in the Snow

Silent whispers on the ground,
Footprints left without a sound.
Paths that twist and turn away,
In the snow, our hearts do sway.

Each impression tells a tale,
Of wanderings, we prevail.
Solitude in white-clad bliss,
In the quiet, find our kiss.

Snowflakes fall like gentle sighs,
Painting dreams across the skies.
With each step, we carve our fate,
In the stillness, contemplate.

Solitary journeys grow,
With the paths we choose to show.
Every print, a memory,
In the snow, we wander free.

So let the winter guide our feet,
In the cold, we feel the heat.
Solitary, yet not alone,
In the snow, our love is shown.

The Solitary Dance of Snowflakes

Falling gently from the sky,
Snowflakes twirl, they float and fly.
In their dance, a story spun,
Each a bright and shining one.

Whispers of a winter's grace,
In the silence, find our place.
Twisting, turning, free in air,
A solitary, lovely flare.

With each flake, a wish bestowed,
In the cold, our hearts erode.
Dancing softly, light and free,
In their movement, we can see.

In the quiet, frosty air,
Snowflakes twirl without a care.
Ever changing, yet the same,
In their beauty, find the flame.

So let us join this timeless waltz,
In the winter's grasp, no faults.
The solitary dance invites,
In the snow, our spirit lights.

A Frozen Reflection of Time

In the stillness, moments freeze,
Echoes dance on winter's breeze.
Silent whispers of the past,
Captured memories, flickers cast.

Glistening paths of crystal light,
Chasing shadows of the night.
Time encased in frosty shields,
In this realm, the heart reveals.

Each breath visible, a fleeting ghost,
In this chill, we ponder most.
The mirror shows a fleeting grace,
Within the ice, the soul's embrace.

Frosted dreams on tarnished ground,
Layers of memories abound.
Perceptions shift as seasons fade,
In frozen beauty, hopes are laid.

A time suspended, never lost,
In quiet depths, we ponder cost.
Every moment, crisp and clear,
A reflection held, forever near.

Shadows Cast by a Pale Sun

Beneath the sky, a muted glow,
Whispers linger, soft and slow.
Shadows stretch across the land,
Silent echoes, hand in hand.

The sun retreats, a timid friend,
As darkness looms, the day can bend.
Fleeting light, a ghostly charm,
Holding tight with quiet harm.

Figures dance on fractured ground,
In the twilight, solace found.
Fragile forms in light's embrace,
Adrift in warmth, a fleeting space.

Each step creates a storynew,
Born of light but shadowed too.
Unyielding paths we dare to tread,
Bearing truths we dare to shed.

In the glow of fading day,
Shadows linger, come what may.
A journey taken, hearts aligned,
In the dance of light, we're blind.

Resilient Hearts Against the Unyielding Cold

Against the chill, our spirits rise,
Fires flicker, warmth defies.
Beneath the weight of winter's breath,
We stand firm, defying death.

Every heartbeat echoes strong,
A melody that stirs along.
In frozen fields, we plant our seeds,
Nurtured hopes fulfill our needs.

Through the frost, we carve our way,
In darkness, find the light of day.
Gathering strength from icy nights,
Resilience shines, ignites our fights.

Hands clasped tight, we brave the storm,
In unity, our hearts transform.
Even as the tempest rolls,
We shelter dreams, we guard our souls.

With every thaw, new life awakes,
Breaking barriers, fear it shakes.
Together we will forge the path,
Against the cold, we choose our wrath.

A Veil of Silence Over the World

A hush descends, a gentle shroud,
Wrapping the earth in stillness proud.
The world asleep, in shadows cupped,
Where whispers linger, secrets tucked.

In soft embrace, the night unfolds,
Tales unspoken, as time molds.
Quietude reigns, a soothing balm,
In the silence, hearts grow calm.

Stars above in watchful gaze,
Painting dreams in eerie haze.
Each flicker tells a story new,
In this calm, the soul finds view.

The moonlight weaves through branches bare,
Casting spells with tender care.
Stillness holds the breath of night,
In the dark, we find the light.

A veil that shrouds both fear and peace,
In silence, we find love's release.
The world a canvas, quiet, whole,
In shadows deep, we find our soul.

Frosted Echoes of Yesterday's Joy

Frosted whispers in the air,
Laughter dances everywhere.
Memories wrapped in silver threads,
Past joys linger where love treads.

Glimmers fade with morning light,
Yet shadows hold the warmth of night.
Each breath carries a soft refrain,
Echoes of joy, both sweet and plain.

Cold winds weave through the trees,
Invisible paths stir memories.
Heartstrings plucked by gentle snow,
Each flake is a chance to grow.

Time may steal what once was bright,
But in our hearts, the warmth ignites.
Frosted echoes never cease,
They cradle our fragments in peace.

In quiet moments, we will find,
The joy that lingers, intertwined.
Wrapped in memory, soft and clear,
Yesterday's joy will always near.

The Lure of the Crystal-Crowned Woods

In woods adorned with crystal light,
Nature calls beneath the night.
Branches sway like whispered dreams,
Shining bright in silver beams.

A path unfolds where shadows dance,
Inviting hearts to take a chance.
Each step leads to a hidden glade,
Where hopes and wishes are remade.

The trees stand tall, a timeless guard,
With secrets kept, their holds are hard.
Within their arms, the world feels new,
Every sigh reveals a clue.

Moonlight filters through the leaves,
Stitching tales that nature weaves.
In this realm, old spirits roam,
Guiding souls toward their home.

The lure of woods calls out so sweet,
With every pulse, the echoes greet.
In crystal crowns, the magic flows,
A timeless dance, where wonder grows.

Ghostly Footprints on a Frozen Shore

On shores where frost meets icy waves,
Ghostly footprints stir like graves.
Silent whispers trace the sand,
Tales of loneliness so grand.

Each step a story left behind,
Winds carry secrets, intertwined.
Footprints fade as tides will rise,
Yet memories linger, never lie.

Footfalls echo through the cold,
In shadows, ancient tales unfold.
A spectral dance of ebb and flow,
Where time stands still, both fast and slow.

Beneath the stars, the silence glows,
With every breath, the coolness grows.
Each wave caresses the stories told,
Of lost spirits in the night so bold.

Yet in this void, we find a spark,
As beauty blooms from the stark.
Ghostly footprints lead us home,
To where our hearts are free to roam.

Dreaming Beneath a Tinsel Sky

Beneath a sky of shimmering dreams,
A tapestry woven with silver beams.
Each star twinkles with whispered grace,
Inviting us to join the chase.

A lullaby hums through the night,
Cradling hopes in soft moonlight.
Every dream a tale to tell,
In the heart where wishes dwell.

Clouds like cotton candy swirl,
Draping the world in a cozy pearl.
We drift through realms of bright delight,
Chasing stardust in our flight.

The tinsel sky beckons us near,
Filling our souls with joy and cheer.
With every heartbeat, magic grows,
Dreams take wing, like fresh-fallen snow.

In this realm of endless night,
We find our strength, we find our light.
Beneath the vast, enchanting sky,
We learn to dream, and we can fly.

The Stillness of Icy Midnight

The moon whispers secrets, soft and low,
Draped in a blanket of glimmering snow.
Tree branches shiver, kissed by the frost,
In the stillness of night, all sense of time is lost.

Shadows dance lightly, in dreams they play,
Echoes of silence where night claims the day.
Stars twinkle brightly, like jewels in the dark,
Each breath a promise, igniting a spark.

The chilly air hums with a mystical tune,
Wrapped in the magic that comes from the moon.
Nature holds its breath, in reverent pause,
In the stillness of midnight, a moment to cause.

The heartbeats of winter, in sync with the night,
Hold onto the calm, let go of the fight.
As time drifts away, under heaven's expanse,
The icy embrace invites you to dance.

Together we linger, in this frozen embrace,
Finding the beauty in the still, quiet space.
Where whispers of nature and dreams intertwine,
In the stillness of icy midnight, we find the divine.

Luminous Shadows in a Pale Landscape

Morning awakens in pastel hues,
Shadows stretch long, dispersing the blues.
Soft light blankets fields, gold and gray,
In this pale landscape, dreams start to play.

Mountains in the distance, kissed by the sun,
Whispers of silence, where day has begun.
The dew on the grass sparkles like gems,
In the luminous glow, the world transcends.

Trees stand in stillness, guardians so grand,
Beneath their branches, the quiet does stand.
Nature's canvas painted with exquisite care,
Luminous shadows dance in the air.

Birdsong breaks gently, a sweet serenade,
Filling the stillness, a moment displayed.
In this tranquil expanse, each heartbeat we share,
Luminous shadows weave magic in the air.

Beneath furls of mist, the earth seems to sigh,
In a pale landscape, where spirits may fly.
With each ray of sunlight, the soul comes to light,
In luminous shadows, our hearts feel the flight.

Allure of the Crystal-Capped Dusk

The sun dips low, painting skies in gold,
As night softly whispers, secrets unfold.
Crystal-capped treetops, aglow in the light,
Allure of the dusk, a magical sight.

Twilight beckons with a gentle embrace,
Colors collide in a delicate space.
The world transforms, as shadows grow tall,
In the allure of dusk, we surrender to all.

Soft breezes rustle, carrying a tune,
Moonbeams emerge, chasing away the gloom.
Stars start to shimmer, one by one,
In this crystal-capped beauty, day is undone.

Whispers of twilight wrap the land tight,
Hints of the dreams that will flow through the night.
In the calm of this hour, let worries disperse,
For in the allure of dusk, the universe nurses.

As day meets the night in a dance so divine,
Every moment suspended, a touch of the spine.
In crystal-capped magic, our spirits will soar,
Drawn in by the dusk, forever wanting more.

Tranquility in a Snow-Draped World

Silent flakes tumble, soft as a sigh,
Transforming the earth where shadows lie.
Covered in white, the world finds its peace,
In tranquility's grip, all worries cease.

Footsteps are muffled, the air crisp and clear,
Nature hums softly, inviting us near.
Branches bow low, adorned like a crown,
In this snow-draped world, beauty astounds.

Whispers of winter float on the breeze,
Embracing the stillness beneath ancient trees.
Each flake tells stories of moments long past,
In tranquility's net, we find love that lasts.

A canvas so pure, where the heart can unwind,
With each gentle snowfall, new dreams we find.
In the hush of the moment, we learn to believe,
In tranquility's hold, the spirit takes leave.

So let us wander in this serene land,
Feeling the magic of winter's soft hand.
In a snow-draped world, where peace reigns supreme,
We gather our thoughts, and in silence, we dream.

Solitude Wrapped in a Blanket of Snow

In quiet flurries, the world slows down,
Each flake a whisper on the frozen ground.
Silence blankets all, a soft, white veil,
In solitude's arms, I set my sail.

The trees stand tall, in their frosty attire,
Glistening under a sun's shy fire.
Footsteps fade in a shimmering trance,
Nature sings softly, inviting the dance.

A distant echo of laughter, a sigh,
The wind carries secrets, low and high.
Each breath I take, crisp and deep,
In solitude's comfort, my heart will keep.

While shadows stretch and daylight wanes,
A chill in the air, the softest chains.
Wrapped in stillness, transformed in glow,
I find my solace; peace in the snow.

A Solitary Star Over a Frostbitten Expanse

In the midnight sky, a star stands alone,
Over frozen fields, it's quietly sown.
A beacon of hope in the velvet night,
Glistening softly, a wondrous sight.

The moon casts shadows on silvery snow,
Whispers of dreams in the cold winds blow.
A lone wanderer beneath the vast sky,
With the star as a guide, I dare to fly.

Frost-kissed branches reach up to the dark,
Seeking the glow of that shimmering spark.
In the expanse, where the chill winds sweep,
I find my thoughts in the stillness deep.

Moments of clarity in cold air's embrace,
The universe whispers in infinite space.
Each twinkle a promise, waiting to be,
In this frosted realm, I long to be free.

With every heartbeat, the night draws near,
That solitary star, forever clear.
In the vastness of night, I feel its warmth,
Guided by light, in solitude's charm.

The Whisper of Winter's Embrace

Winter whispers softly, soft as a sigh,
Blanketing valleys as the cold winds fly.
Each gust carries tales from days gone by,
In nature's hush, all echoes awry.

Branches adorned with crystals like lace,
Twinkling under a moonlit embrace.
The world, untouched, in slumber's soft hold,
In winter's arms, I feel the bold.

Footprints forgotten in the hush of snow,
Memories linger where only dreams flow.
The air is crisp like freshly held breath,
In winter's embrace, I ponder death.

Yet in the silence, there's beauty profound,
Life stirs beneath where hope can be found.
With every flake that dances and sways,
Winter whispers gently, counting the days.

Each falling snowflake, a story retold,
Of warmth and of solace amid the cold.
In the tapestry woven of ice and of night,
Winter's soft whisper brings shadows to light.

Lullabies of a Lost Frosted Horizon

In the stillness of night, a lullaby hums,
A frosted horizon where stillness becomes.
Each breath a whisper, serene and clear,
As echoes of twilight drift gently near.

The sky, a canvas of silver and gray,
Holds the promise of night, as shadows play.
Lost in the beauty of winter's soft glow,
Lullabies drift where the cold winds blow.

Frosted trees sway with a silent grace,
Their branches like fingers tracing the space.
Stars twinkle bright in the frosty dome,
Guiding the dreamers who wander from home.

In this enchanted realm, dreams take flight,
As the moon casts shadows, silvery white.
A symphony played in a hushed refrain,
Whispers of warmth amid winter's domain.

Each note a memory, soft and profound,
In the lullabies lost, the heart can be found.
Embraced by the night as the world holds its breath,
In the frost-bitten whispers, I dance with death.

Lament of the Lost Leaves

Once bright banners, now they fade,
Whispers of life in the cool shade.
Dancing softly in the breeze,
Memories caught in the dying trees.

Crimson dreams in the autumn air,
Scattered dreams without a care.
Fallen warriors, they rest in peace,
In the silence, their sorrows cease.

Each leaf a story, a moment's grace,
Now forgotten in nature's embrace.
The ground is rich with their gentle sighs,
As the winds carry their soft goodbyes.

Through the chaos of the changing night,
They drift away, lost from sight.
Yet in the heart, their beauty stays,
In whispered thoughts of golden days.

In the stillness, we mourn and sigh,
For the lost leaves that once could fly.
Nature's cycle, endless and free,
Still, we grieve for what used to be.

The Stillness of Evening Snow

Silent flakes in soft descent,
Wrapping the world in a calm event.
Each petal cold, yet warm in hue,
A blanket thick with dreams anew.

Footprints vanish in the white,
Lost to shadows, lost from sight.
Whispers caught in the frosty air,
Secrets linger, soft and rare.

Moonlight dances on crystal ground,
In this stillness, peace is found.
Time stands still amidst the glow,
In the beauty of evening snow.

Beneath the surface, life waits still,
Nature's heartbeat, a gentle thrill.
In quietude, we find our home,
In the silence, we're free to roam.

When dawn arrives with rosy light,
The world awakes, gleaming bright.
Yet in our hearts, the stillness stays,
In evening's snow, we count the days.

Shimmering Silence of the Bare Trees

Branches reaching, stark and tall,
In winter's grip, they stand enthralled.
Covered in frost, they hold their breath,
In shimmering silence, they dance with death.

Leaves long gone, with tales untold,
Their secrets lie in the bitter cold.
Each knotted limb tells a story rare,
In the still of winter, they lay bare.

Moonlight spills on their fragile form,
Casting shadows, gentle and warm.
Rustling whispers in the night,
A ballet of frost in soft moonlight.

Time may wear their edges thin,
Yet the beauty beneath still lies within.
In their silence, a strength can be found,
A testament to the stillness around.

When spring returns, they'll find their voice,
Swaying softly, they'll rejoice.
But in the winter's gentle plea,
We find solace in their mystery.

Frost-Kissed Memories

Each breath draws whispers of the past,
Where shadows linger, memories cast.
Frost-kissed visions in morning's light,
Echoes of laughter, fleeting and bright.

Time's passage graced by icy touch,
In tender moments, we remember much.
Captured glimmers in the heart's embrace,
Frozen fragments of time and space.

The world transformed by a chilly gleam,
Suspended reality, a waking dream.
In the frost, we find lost names,
Mapped in silence, their fleeting flames.

Nature cradles these echoes near,
In soft shivers, a pang of cheer.
Each frost-kissed moment, a gentle sigh,
A reminder of why we still fly high.

When the sun warms the frozen ground,
We hold these memories, tightly bound.
Though seasons change and time moves fast,
In frost-kissed dreams, we everlast.

Solitude in the Whisper of Snowflakes

Snowflakes drift, pure and light,
Silence wraps the world tight.
Each flake dances on the air,
Whispers secrets, soft and rare.

A blanket white, so serene,
In solitude, a tranquil scene.
Footsteps echo in the deep,
While shadows of the night do creep.

The moon watches from above,
Casting down its gentle love.
Nature's breath, a fleeting pause,
In this moment, time withdrew its claws.

Cold embrace, a sweet retreat,
Where heart and mind can softly meet.
In every drift, a story spun,
Of winter's peace, a world undone.

Solitude, the song it sings,
Wrapped in warmth that silence brings.
Snowflakes whisper their refrain,
In solitude, we find our gain.

Enchantment in a White Wasteland

Endless fields of purest white,
Where dreams take flight in soft twilight.
A wasteland cloaked in winter's grace,
Each crystal spark finds its place.

Beneath the frost, life waits and breathes,
With whispers caught in frozen leaves.
Magic swirls in every flake,
An enchantment no ice can shake.

The quiet hum of nature's tune,
Beneath the watchful, silver moon.
Here in silence, wonders bloom,
In the cold lies untainted room.

Branches bow from heavy loads,
As twilight paints the white abodes.
Footprints mark the paths we tread,
In this wasteland, dreams are fed.

Visions dance on winter's breath,
Finding life in quiet death.
Enchantment sways the weary soul,
In white expanses, we feel whole.

Stories Told in the Chill of Twilight

Twilight whispers as day departs,
Stories weave through softened hearts.
Chill descends, a tender cloak,
Each breath shared, a silent stroke.

Across the horizon, shadows play,
Painting tales in shades of gray.
Fingers trace the icy air,
Crafting dreams, both light and rare.

Beneath the stars, the world holds tight,
As secrets linger in the night.
Voices murmur, echoes blend,
In twilight's grip, time will suspend.

The chill wraps us like a sigh,
As stories swirl and spirits fly.
In every glance, a tale reborn,
In the cool, our hearts are worn.

Life unfolds in shadows cast,
In the twilight, we hold fast.
Stories told in every breath,
In the chill, we dance with death.

Shimmering Silence of a Snow-Blanketed Dawn

Morning breaks in shimmering light,
Snow-blanketed world, pure delight.
Silence reigns, a sacred space,
In this dawn, we find our grace.

Each gleaming flake, a star reborn,
As dawn unfolds, the day is sworn.
Gentle whispers grace the trees,
In stillness, we feel the breeze.

Soft hues paint the endless sky,
Where clouds drift and memories lie.
A tranquil hush, the world awakes,
With every breath, the silence quakes.

Moments lost in time's embrace,
Shimmering paths, a whispered chase.
Echoes of the night retreat,
As dawn unfolds, we feel complete.

In this silence, hope ignites,
Beneath the blanket, dreams take flight.
Snow-blanketed serenity,
In dawn's embrace, we long to be.

Glimmers of Light on Snowy Hills

Softly the sunlight kisses the snow,
Glimmers of warmth in a world aglow.
Footprints dance lightly upon the white,
Nature's own canvas, a pure delight.

Whispers of wind through branches sway,
A symphony plays as the skies turn gray.
Curves of the hills beneath clouds bright,
Chasing the shadows, embracing the light.

Children laugh, their cheeks all aglow,
Building their dreams in the soft, pure glow.
Winter's embrace, a magical thrill,
Glimmers of beauty on snowy hill.

Sunset ignites the horizon wide,
Painting the canvas as daylight died.
Moments of wonder, stillness so bright,
Glimmers of light on a magical night.

Reflections in a Glittering Pond

Under the surface, the world shines clear,
Reflections of dreams that we hold dear.
Ripples dance lightly, a gentle play,
Whispers of nature softly convey.

Willows bend low, kissing the stream,
Mirrored visions blend with a dream.
Colors collide in a soft embrace,
Each moment captured, a quiet grace.

Frogs serenade in the twilight glow,
As stars awaken, their soft light flows.
Every small wave tells a tale anew,
Reflections of life in the evening dew.

Gentle breezes stir the cool night air,
Nature's soft choir sings everywhere.
Peacefully drifting, as time slips on,
Reflections shimmer till the light is gone.

Emptiness Wrapped in White

A hush blankets all in the still of night,
Emptiness wrapped in a cloak of white.
Silent echoes linger in the air,
Cold and serene, a moment to spare.

Curled up in dreams, the world is asleep,
Secrets are hidden in silence, so deep.
Snowflakes drift softly, the night's sweet art,
Whispers of winter, a quiet heart.

Footsteps erased in a shroud of snow,
All of the noise of the day laid low.
Lost in the silence, the shadows play,
Emptiness sings, and night holds sway.

Where laughter once echoed and colors shone,
Now solitude reigns in a world alone.
Yet in this stillness, a beauty unfolds,
Emptiness wrapped in white, the heart beholds.

Chill of the Twilight Hour

As the day surrenders to night's soft call,
The chill of twilight embraces us all.
Sky painted lilac, a fleeting show,
Nature prepares for a world turned slow.

Leaves rustle gently in fading light,
Shapes melt away into the coming night.
Each breath hangs heavy on the crisp air,
Whispers of silence linger everywhere.

The moon timidly peeks from behind the veil,
Stars glimmer softly, with stories to tell.
Shadows grow longer, a dance with the dark,
Chill of the twilight, a quiet spark.

As night envelopes, the world takes a pause,
Resting in peace, without any cause.
Twilight's embrace, a gentle bow,
Caught in the chill of this solemn hour.

Whispers Between the Flakes

Softly falling from the gray,
Snowflakes dance in silent play.
Each one tells a secret new,
Whispers carried on the dew.

In the hush of winter's breath,
Flakes descend, a gentle death.
Nature's quilt, so pure, so white,
Blankets all in quiet light.

Trees stand tall, their arms so bare,
Cradling dreams in chilly air.
Every flake a whispered sigh,
Soon to melt and say goodbye.

Footprints lost in drifts so deep,
While the world begins to sleep.
Winter's heart beats slow and calm,
In its chill, there's subtle balm.

Underneath the moon's soft glow,
Flakes keep falling, ever slow.
In the night, a world transforms,
Within its grasp, all beauty warms.

The Taste of Cold Solitude

Beneath the vast and chilling sky,
I wander where the shadows lie.
Each breath a cloud in frosty air,
In solitude, I find my care.

Whispers drift on icy streams,
Lonesome echoes of lost dreams.
The silence wraps like winter's shawl,
In the stillness, I hear it call.

Footsteps crunch on crunchy ground,
Every sound a hallowed bound.
In the distance, a lonely owl,
Sings a song of the night's scowl.

Snowflakes twirl, a graceful dance,
In this quiet, I take my chance.
The taste of cold, a bitter sweet,
In this moment, I am complete.

As stars emerge, a glimmer bright,
Guiding me through the endless night.
Within the frost, I find my peace,
In the hush, my sorrows cease.

Silent Frost on Shadowed Trails

On pathways where the wild winds roam,
Silent frost finds a place called home.
Every step leaves a story told,
In the chill, the world turns bold.

Moonlight spills on the frozen ground,
In the quiet, lost souls found.
Whispers linger in the trees,
Carried softly by the breeze.

Tracks of beasts in silver sheen,
In the night, where few have been.
Each breath visible, crisp and clear,
Through the silence, I have no fear.

Branches groan, the cold they bear,
Nature's canvas, beyond compare.
Frosty lace on every twig,
A tranquil dance—a gentle jig.

As dawn breaks with colors bright,
I find warmth in the morning light.
Silent frost fades with the day,
Yet its magic will always stay.

Whispers of the Frostbitten Breeze

Through the night, the cold winds sigh,
Whispers low as they drift by.
Frostbitten tales the shadows weave,
In their magic, we believe.

Branches sway in a silent dance,
Underneath the moon's soft glance.
Every gust, a gentle tease,
Carrying secrets on the freeze.

Amidst the chill, memories beckon,
Each icy breath a soul's connection.
Nature speaks in hushed poet's tone,
In every flake, I find my own.

Footfalls echoed on white trails,
Rustling leaves tell wondrous tales.
In this stillness, life feels grand,
Touched by winter's unseen hand.

As dawn awakens, colors blend,
Frostbitten whispers start to mend.
In the wake of the morning bloom,
I find solace in the room.

The Lonely Flicker of a Hearth's Light

In the corner, shadows dance,
A flicker warms the cold room's stance.
Each flickering flame a silent sigh,
Whispers of stories, forgotten by and by.

Cinders settling with weary grace,
Beneath the ember's soft embrace.
Night drapes the world in its velvety cloak,
While the hearth hums gently, a life spoke.

In solitude, a heart finds peace,
As surrounding chaos finds release.
The gentle glow, a calming friend,
In its warm gaze, the worries mend.

Time drips slowly, a flooded well,
Words unspoken begin to dwell.
Within the hearth's light, dreams bide,
As memories find warmth inside.

To the lonely flicker, we heed its call,
In this quiet space, we rise or fall.
Each heartbeat synced to fire's play,
In the hearth's glow, we find our way.

Serenity Wrapped in a Shroud of Snow

Gentle flakes fall from skies so gray,
Blanketing whispers, the world's far away.
Each soft touch, a moment of grace,
In the silence, nature finds its place.

Trees draped in white, a soft embrace,
Crystal branches, a delicate lace.
Footsteps muffled, thoughts free to roam,
In this peaceful hush, we find our home.

The world transformed, a canvas bright,
Underneath stars that twinkle at night.
Every breath hangs like a dream,
In this snowy realm, life is a stream.

In the distance, whispers of delight,
Winter's charm lingers in the light.
Wrapped in serenity, hearts do sing,
While snowflakes dance, enchanting spring.

Bound by the beauty, in silence we grow,
Finding our solace in the falling snow.
Nature's embrace, a soft lullaby,
In this tranquil space, our spirits fly.

Glinting Memories Beneath a Frozen Canopy

Beneath branches aglow with icy sheen,
Whispers of history, serene yet keen.
Echoes of laughter, shadows of cheer,
In the frost-tinged air, the past is near.

A tapestry woven in silver threads,
Memories linger, where the past treads.
Each step crackles, a story unfolds,
As the heart recalls what time once holds.

Frozen silhouettes dance in the light,
Ghosts of the moments, cherished and bright.
Under the canopy, dreams intertwine,
Glinting reflections of love's design.

From each glimmer, a tale to tell,
Of joys and sorrows, a bittersweet spell.
In the cold, warmth lingers on high,
Beneath the frost, the soul learns to fly.

Carried by winds that softly call,
In memories, we rise or we fall.
Glinting memories beneath it all,
In frozen embrace, we stand tall.

The Sigh of Stars Through Chilling Air

Above, a tapestry of dreams unfold,
Stars whisper stories, ancient and bold.
In the stillness, a breath of night,
Each twinkle carries a glimmering light.

The chill wraps tightly, a cloak to wear,
Yet hope glimmers in the midnight air.
A sigh escapes, a fleeting thought,
Connected by cosmos, all that we sought.

In the darkness, a canvas stretched wide,
Galaxies twirling, an endless ride.
With every blink, a wish takes flight,
In the chill of night, we find our might.

Voices of starlight sing to the moon,
In quiet hours, we become in tune.
Under the heavens, dreams take their stand,
The sigh of stars, a soothing hand.

In chilling air, the universe glows,
A reminder that magic forever flows.
To reach for the stars, we dare to aspire,
Through the night, we ignite our fire.

Graceful Shadows in Frigid Glow

In the night, shadows weave,
Soft whispers in the cold.
Moonlight spills on frosted leaves,
A story gently told.

Graceful forms, they sway and glide,
Carried by the winter's breath.
In stillness, hearts and dreams collide,
Finding peace in frigid depth.

Winds sing softly through the trees,
Each note a fleeting sigh.
Mysteries float on icy breeze,
As time slips quietly by.

Footprints lost; the world unwinds,
In shadows, warmth will find.
Whispers linger, love entwined,
Forever intertwined.

In the dark, the heart will glow,
Wrapped in winter's soft embrace.
Dance with shadows, let love show,
In this frigid, sacred place.

The Silent Dance of Falling Snow

Snowflakes twirl, a silent waltz,
Gentle grace in purest white.
They kiss the ground, without a fault,
Turning day to soft twilight.

Each crystal holds a fleeting dream,
Capturing the chill of night.
Underneath the silver beam,
The world is cloaked in quiet light.

Whispers of the falling dust,
Blanket all with tender care.
In this moment, still we trust,
Life is sweet, and time is rare.

Footsteps hush, the pulse slows down,
Every breath a cloud of ghost.
In silence glows a silver crown,
Nature's beauty, we love most.

As snowflakes dance, we stand in awe,
Captivated by their flight.
Life's fragile grace is nature's law,
In this dream-like, soft twilight.

Memories Cradled in Icy Stillness

Frozen echoes in the air,
Whispers of what once has been.
Moments linger everywhere,
In the hush of winter's sheen.

Each breath carries tales untold,
Echoing in the frosty night.
In the cold, our dreams unfold,
Wrapped in soft, ethereal light.

Footsteps trace a distant way,
In the past, we dance and sway.
Through the frost, they gently play,
Guiding hearts that yearn to stay.

Time's embrace, a gentle hold,
Cradles memories with care.
In the icy grasp, we behold,
Love like fire, frozen air.

From the depths, the warmth will rise,
In the stillness, joy will gleam.
Icy drapes, adorned with sighs,
Cradle softly every dream.

Fragments of Light in a Solemn Abyss

In shadows deep, the heart takes flight,
Amidst the dark, a spark ignites.
Fragments of hope, shining bright,
Illuminate the silent nights.

Lost in depths, where echoes drown,
Whispers weave through the dismay.
In the quiet, we reclaim our crown,
Finding strength in cold decay.

Every shard of light we trace,
Guides us through the heavy gloom.
In despair, we find our place,
Transforming struggle into bloom.

Though the abyss may seem unkind,
Flickering flames will ignite the way.
In our hearts, a fire entwined,
Brings the dawn of another day.

Together, we mend the broken seams,
In darkness, we will stand and fight.
Fragments of love weave through our dreams,
Illuminating the endless night.

Echoes Beneath a Shimmering Veil

In twilight's glow, whispers play,
Dreams dance softly, fading away.
Beneath the stars, shadows blend,
Where secrets of the night transcend.

Rippling waters reflect the sight,
A mirror to the lost daylight.
Each echo calls in soft refrain,
A lullaby of joy and pain.

Moonbeams trace the silent ground,
In their embrace, solace is found.
The heartbeats thrumming, felt so clear,
As nature's voice draws ever near.

In hidden nooks, mysteries grow,
Beneath the veil of silver glow.
While night's gentle fingers weave,
The tales that only stars believe.

The Embrace of a Glistening Twilight

As daylight bows, shadows entwine,
A canvas painted, soft and fine.
With every breath, the stillness sighs,
In the embrace of twilight skies.

Colors bleed and gently fade,
Where dreams emerge, unafraid.
Each fleeting moment, pure delight,
Underneath the cloak of night.

Soft whispers drift from hidden trees,
Carried on the evening breeze.
Nature hums its quiet tune,
As stars awaken, one by one.

The world finds peace, a moment's rest,
In the twilight's gentle vest.
Hold my hand, let time stand still,
As we dance upon the hill.

Hushed Pines and Shy Moonlight

In the forest, whispers blend,
Hushed pines watch as shadows send.
Moonlight drapes in silver lace,
Embracing night with gentle grace.

Each branch sways with secrets bold,
In the darkness, stories told.
A shy moon peeks through leafy veil,
Guiding dreams where spirits sail.

Softly glistening, dew drops fall,
Nature's silence, a soothing call.
While owls sing their lullabies,
Underneath the starlit skies.

Echoes of a distant pine,
Kissing thoughts, so sweet, divine.
In tender night, we find our way,
Through hushed pines, where shadows play.

When the World Slumbers in White

When winter's breath wraps all around,
A blanket soft, without a sound.
In slumber deep, the earth will dream,
A world of wonders, pure and gleam.

Snowflakes dance on chilly air,
Whispers float, a frosty prayer.
Yet in their fall, the stillness sighs,
While the quiet night slowly lies.

Each tree is draped in icy light,
Holding secrets of the night.
The moon above, a sentinel,
Watching over, soft and well.

In every flake, a story's spun,
Of sunlit days and evening sun.
As dreams take flight on winter's breath,
We embrace the beauty of this depth.

Shadows Beneath the Icicles

Hanging low, the icicles gleam,
Casting shadows like a dream.
Beneath their weight, the silence grows,
Whispers echo where the frost blows.

Darkened corners hold their breath,
Wrapped in the chill of a quiet death.
The world outside moves fast and bright,
While shadows linger in muted light.

Time itself appears to freeze,
Memories dance upon the breeze.
In the stillness, hearts entwine,
Finding warmth in the cold so divine.

Melting drops create a symphony,
Each note a fleeting memory.
The sunlight pierces through the gray,
Revealing colors in disarray.

Yet in the cracks of winter's might,
Hope flickers softly, pure and bright.
For beneath the weight of icy fears,
Lies the promise of spring's warm tears.

Solitude Beneath the Silent Sky

Underneath the vast expanse,
Lonely stars seem to dance.
A whisper floats on the night air,
In solitude, we lay bare.

The moon watches from on high,
Casting visions as time slips by.
In this quiet, hearts take flight,
Bound by dreams in the still of night.

Clouds drift slowly, a silver veil,
While shadows weave a haunting tale.
Echoes murmur through the trees,
In the silence, we find peace.

Beneath the sky so deep and wide,
Thoughts retreat with the moon as guide.
In the chill of night, we discover,
The beauty of time spent with another.

For in this realm of starry skies,
Solitude brings the sweetest sighs.
In stillness, our spirits embrace,
Finding solace in this sacred space.

An Intimate Chill

Frosty breath hangs in the air,
In the stillness, hearts lay bare.
A gentle touch, a fleeting sigh,
Love lingers as the moments fly.

Whispers soft as falling snow,
Every secret feels like a glow.
In the chill, connections spark,
Lighting warmth in the deepest dark.

Tangled hands, a delicate dance,
Lost in each other's glance.
The world fades, it's just us two,
In this intimate space, pure and true.

Winter wraps us in its fold,
Our laughter breaks the biting cold.
In this quiet, we find our way,
Crafting warmth amidst the gray.

So let the chill embrace us whole,
As we weave the threads of our soul.
Together here, we find our thrill,
In the beauty of an intimate chill.

The Solace of the Snowfall

Gently falling, snowflakes twirled,
Blanketing the quiet world.
Each flake whispers tales untold,
In white, the dark feels less bold.

Silence wraps the earth in light,
As winter's calm quells the night.
Footsteps muffled, soft and slow,
In this stillness, peace can grow.

Nature's hush, a soothing balm,
In the chaos, find the calm.
Every flake falls like a prayer,
Holding dreams in the frosty air.

Children laugh, creating cheer,
While winter's beauty draws us near.
Each snowman built, a joyful mark,
In the dance of snow after dark.

Together, we embrace the snow,
In its solace, let our worries go.
With every flurry that fills the sky,
We find warmth where the cold winds sigh.

The Absence of Sound in Stillness

In the hush of nightfall's grace,
Whispers vanish, lost in space.
The world pauses, breath held tight,
Crickets cease, the stars ignite.

A gentle breeze, a fleeting sigh,
Leaves dance slowly, dreams drift by.
Moonlight glimmers on quiet seas,
Time stands still, in perfect ease.

Echoes fade, a soft retreat,
Silent shadows, soft and neat.
Footsteps muted on the ground,
In this void, peace becomes profound.

Sorrow Wrapped in Snow

Under blankets of white despair,
Memories linger in the air.
Each flake falls, a tear from skies,
Grief whispers as the night complies.

Branches weep, their burdens wane,
Frozen petals, frozen pain.
The world asleep in winter's keep,
Heartbeats hushed where secrets seep.

Silent streets where shadows creep,
Lonely echoes that weep and weep.
In the silence, hope can grow,
Life awaits beneath the snow.

A Quiet Respite from the World

Amid the chaos, find your space,
A hidden nook, a sacred place.
Where worries drift like autumn leaves,
And only peace in silence weaves.

Soft sunlight spills through window frames,
Whispers of dreams call out by names.
With every breath, the heart finds rest,
A quiet moment, truly blessed.

Time slows down, the mind takes flight,
In gentle hues of morning light.
For in this calm, the soul is free,
To dance with thoughts, to simply be.

Still Faces of Frozen Waters

Beneath the ice, the world is slow,
Reflecting dreams in silver glow.
Each ripple holds a secret's grip,
In cold embrace, the shadows slip.

Silent reflections whisper low,
Visions play in winter's show.
The stillness speaks, as heartbeats pause,
Nature's artwork, full of flaws.

In frozen depths, the stories weave,
Hushed promises that we believe.
Still faces of the waters sleep,
In tranquil depths, their secrets keep.

Reverie in Crystal Clarity

In dreams I wander, softly caught,
A world of whispers, gently bought.
Bright shards of light in endless sky,
Where time drifts slow, and shadows fly.

Each thought a feather, light and free,
In crystal clarity, I see.
A fleeting touch of what could be,
Reflections dance, a mystery.

With every breath, the silence hums,
A melody that softly comes.
In reveries, my heart takes flight,
Embraced by peace of pure delight.

The colors blend, a tranquil hue,
As dreams unfold, both bright and true.
In this embrace, I find my place,
In whispers of the cosmic grace.

So let the world just fade away,
In crystal clarity, I stay.
A realm of thought, serene and bright,
Where day meets night, in softest light.

Alone with the Winter Winds

The chill wraps round, a velvet cloak,
Where silence waits and shadows poke.
Each breath a cloud, a fleeting thought,
In winter's grasp, the warmth is sought.

Frosted whispers kiss the trees,
With every sigh, the world will freeze.
The wind it howls, a ghostly song,
In solitude, I feel so strong.

Snowflakes twirl like dancers high,
In stillness deep, beneath the sky.
I watch the world turn white and gray,
As winter winds weave soft ballet.

Time slows down in icy breath,
Each moment holds a hint of death.
Yet here I stand, alive, awake,
Embracing all these storms I make.

With every gust, I find my core,
In solitude, I long for more.
The winter's chill, a fierce embrace,
Alone with winds, I find my space.

The Comfort of Isolated Nights

Stars sprinkle dreams across the dark,
Each twinkle shines, a silent spark.
In isolation, warmth I find,
A quiet peace, a forward mind.

Wrapped in shadows, I breathe deep,
The world outside, a dreamless sleep.
Here in this calm, my heart takes wing,
In isolated nights, my thoughts take spring.

The moonlight bathes the world in grace,
In solitude, I find my place.
With every sigh, the night unfolds,
A tapestry of tales untold.

The tick of time becomes a friend,
In quiet moments, pain can mend.
Each whisper soft, each heartbeat true,
In isolation, I find the new.

So let the stars be my embrace,
In comfort found, a sacred space.
These isolated nights, my gentle muse,
In quietude, there's much to choose.

Craig of the Cloaked Silence

A mountain stands in solemn grace,
Where whispers dwell, a hidden place.
The craig looms high, a guardian still,
In cloaked silence, it bends to will.

Each stone a story, old and wise,
Beneath the gaze of endless skies.
Time does not rush, nor does it bow,
In quietude, I breathe somehow.

Lost to the world, yet found within,
The silence wraps like gentle skin.
Here echoes fade, like dreams once sown,
In solitude, I feel at home.

The shadows stretch, the light grows dim,
With every pulse, my thoughts begin.
In cloaked silence, I touch the deep,
Where secrets rest, and sorrows sleep.

The craig stands firm through night and day,
In silent watch, it keeps decay.
A timeless space where heartbeats blend,
In solitude, the soul ascends.

The Still Heartbeat of Nature's Rest

In quiet woods, the shadows fall,
Where whispers dance and silence calls.
The gentle breeze sings soft and low,
As stars above begin to glow.

The moonlight paints the sleeping land,
A silver cloak, both light and grand.
The rustle of the leaves, a sigh,
Beneath the watchful, starlit sky.

The branches cradle night's sweet tune,
While crickets chirp beneath the moon.
A tranquil hush enfolds the night,
As dreams take wing and take their flight.

With every breath, the world stands still,
As time is marked by nature's will.
In this embrace of peace so deep,
The heart of night begins to sleep.

Awake it waits for dawn's soft light,
To rise and greet the warmer sight.
Yet for now, in stillness found,
The heartbeat rests on sacred ground.

Icy Patterns on the Breath of Dawn

As morning breaks, the frost takes hold,
A crystal quilt, serene and bold.
Each breath a plume, a fleeting trace,
Of winter's kiss on nature's face.

The air is sharp, the world a gleam,
In silken white, a waking dream.
The sun peeks through the silver mist,
Awakening the earth with gentle twist.

Icy branches crack like glass,
Beneath the weight, the shadows pass.
A tranquil scene, so still and pure,
In every glance, a heart to cure.

The patterns dance on every breath,
A fleeting moment before the death.
These whispers of a winter's song,
Remind us all we too belong.

With every glint, a story told,
Of frozen whispers, brave and bold.
In these bright shards, life's truth we find,
Through icy patterns, hearts entwined.

An Odyssey Through Shimmering White

Through drifts of snow, the world awakes,
An odyssey where silence breaks.
Each step we take, a crunch, a sound,
In whiteness deep, with joy unbound.

The frosted trees wear coats of lace,
While crystal sparkles leave their trace.
A path ahead, so bright, so clear,
The journey beckons, drawing near.

In shimmering fields, the sunlight plays,
While shadows dance in winter's haze.
The purity of thoughts, so light,
In every breath, the warmth ignites.

With laughter shared, the moments fly,
As gleeful hearts beneath the sky.
In this bright realm, we wander free,
An odyssey for you and me.

The winding trails, they twist and turn,
Each corner holds a chance to learn.
In shimmering white, we find our way,
Towards tomorrow, come what may.

Gossamer Dreams in the Frozen Hours

In frozen hours, the night unfolds,
With gossamer dreams and tales retold.
The stars like lanterns softly gleam,
Illuminating every dream.

A tapestry of silver hues,
Where whispers float on crystal blues.
In the stillness, magic weaves,
As moonlight dances on the leaves.

The air is thick with echoes faint,
Of secret wishes, soft and quaint.
Each heart a flame, a flicker bright,
As shadows play with fading light.

Through frosted panes, the world is seen,
In crystalline hues, a tranquil sheen.
With every breath, the moments pause,
In frozen hours of nature's cause.

Gossamer dreams on winter's breath,
Reveal the beauty found in death.
Yet through it all, we find a way,
To glimpse the dawn of a new day.

The Memory of a Sunlit Summer

Golden rays danced on the sea,
Laughter and joy, wild and free.
Children played beneath the trees,
A warm embrace in the gentle breeze.

Time slipped by, oh, how it flew,
Moments cherished, memories true.
Sunset hues painted the sky,
As twilight whispered its soft goodbye.

Shadows grew long in the fading light,
Stars appeared, twinkling bright.
Night's cool hand caressed the land,
Holding us close, a silent command.

Those days linger in the heart,
A vivid tapestry, a work of art.
Soft whispers of the past, held tight,
In the stillness of the night.

The memory sings a gentle song,
Of sunlit days that felt so long.
In every ray, in every beam,
Lives the essence of a dream.

Chilled Echoes on an Empty Path

Frosted leaves crunch underfoot,
Morning chill, a quiet pursuit.
Whispers of winter fill the air,
In this stillness, silent prayer.

Bare branches reach for the sky,
A heartbeat lost in a soft sigh.
Shadows dance in dim light,
The world wears a cloak of white.

Footsteps fade in the frozen ground,
Echoes linger, a haunting sound.
A path once vibrant now lies bare,
Chilled echoes whisper everywhere.

Yet in the cold, beauty blooms,
A quiet grace among the glooms.
In every breath, a ghost of heat,
In solitude, cold feels sweet.

Each moment savored, profound and still,
Nature's secrets weave, and fill.
In the silence, peace aligned,
Chilled echoes, a treasure to find.

Serenity Found in the Frosty Embrace

Soft crystals fall from the sky,
Delicate lace where visions lie.
Nature's hush blankets the ground,
In the quiet, solace found.

Breath turns to mist, a gentle sigh,
As winter's spirit passes by.
Trees stand tall, dressed in white,
Guardians of the tranquil night.

Stars twinkle in a frozen sea,
Each a wish, a memory.
The moon casts silver on the snow,
As time stands still, lost in glow.

Here in embrace, I find my peace,
In winter's grace, all worries cease.
Heartbeats match with the night's calm hush,
In this stillness, I feel the rush.

Serenity wrapped in a frosty shroud,
In every silence, the world feels proud.
A gentle kiss from the winter's breath,
In this moment, I feel no death.

A Wrapped Gift of Resilient Stillness

In the quiet of dawn, hope awakes,
Wrapped in stillness, the world breaks.
Tender light spills from the sky,
A promise hidden in the shy.

Each moment holds a gentle grace,
A wrapped gift in time and space.
Through the chaos, peace will find,
A sanctuary for the mind.

Nature's rhythm, soft and slow,
In every heartbeat, resilience grows.
With every shadow the light will chase,
In stillness lies a calming place.

Leaves flutter softly, whispers low,
Tales of strength in ebb and flow.
In each breeze, a secret spun,
The dance of life has just begun.

A moment to breathe, a chance to feel,
In wrapped stillness, the heart can heal.
In every pause, we find our way,
Resilient souls here to stay.

Luminescence of a Darkened Dawn

In shadows deep, the night holds tight,
Stars flicker low, preparing flight.
Yet the horizon whispers low,
A hint of light begins to glow.

Clouds drift softly, a velvet shroud,
Veiling dreams beneath a crowd.
Crimson blush on distant hills,
Awakening the world that chills.

Echoes of dawn, a soft embrace,
Filling the void, a tranquil space.
The beauty lies in stillness shown,
As night retreats to realms unknown.

With every breath, the day takes hold,
A tapestry of hues unfolds.
The luminescence warms the ground,
In whispered tones, hope is found.

Emerging light, so pure, so bright,
Chasing away the leftover fright.
In darkened hours, there's always grace,
A dawn that paints with softest trace.

Frostbound Reverie

Silent night wraps the world in white,
Each flake dances, a twinkling light.
The air is crisp, a biting chill,
Yet in this cold, the heart stands still.

Trees wear crowns of icy lace,
Nature's art, a frozen grace.
Whispers of winter, soft and clear,
Echo in the silence we hold dear.

Footsteps crunch on powdered ground,
In the stillness, magic is found.
Underneath the moon's soft glow,
Dreams unfurl in the frostbound flow.

Stars overhead, a shimmering sigh,
As frosty tendrils weave through the sky.
Each breath forms clouds, a fleeting mist,
In this reverie, none can resist.

Time stands still, a tranquil pause,
In the beauty of winter's cause.
With every glance, a story told,
In the frostbound night, the heart turns bold.

Luminary of the Long Night

Through the dark, the moonlight beams,
Casting shadows, whispering dreams.
A luminous guide, so serene,
Watches over the world, unseen.

Stars twinkle like forgotten tales,
In the hush, their soft gleam prevails.
Navigating fears and doubt,
The luminary shines, casting about.

In every heart, a flicker grows,
Illuminating paths, as it flows.
Embrace the night, find your way,
In the silent glow of silver sway.

Time yields to the calming light,
As the world breathes in the night.
With the moon as your steadfast friend,
Let dreams and hopes intertwine and mend.

Darkness cannot swallow what shines,
For the luminary's glow aligns.
In the long night, we find our grace,
As we wander through space's embrace.

Nature's Quiet Quill on Snow

In the hush of winter's breath,
Nature pens with a touch of death.
Each snowflake falls a whispered line,
Writing stories, divine, benign.

Blankets thick, the earth now sleeps,
In icy dreams, deep silence keeps.
The quiet quill, a feathered wisp,
Crafting elegance with each crisp.

Footprints fade, the wild grows still,
As nature writes with unyielding will.
Each stroke captures the essence true,
In whitewashed canvases of hue.

Boughs bow low with tender weight,
Embracing peace, a silent fate.
Underneath the blanket, seeds lay deep,
Awaiting spring when the world will leap.

From frozen ink, new life will spring,
As the thaw brings forth awakening.
Nature's quill writes without haste,
A timeless dance, in stillness traced.

The Ghosts of Leaves Long Gone

In the whispering woods they tread,
Fingers brushing the ground, once fed.
Leaves of amber, gold, now lost,
Mark the seasons, remember the cost.

Beneath the boughs, shadows sway,
Echoes of laughter fade away.
Time's cruel hand has swept them high,
Yet their essence lingers nigh.

Each rustle speaks of stories old,
Of autumns bright and winters cold.
In silence, they share their plight,
The ghosts of leaves, in fading light.

Memories dance on the breeze's sigh,
Songs of the ancients in a soft goodbye.
Nature's canvas, bittersweet hues,
Whispering secrets of cherished views.

Though they've withered, their spirit glows,
In the earth, where the tender heart throes.
Shades of color in twilight's embrace,
Remind us of joy in loss and grace.

Traces of Solitude on Hushed Paths

On winding trails where echoes hush,
Footsteps linger in nature's brush.
Every twist a silent plea,
From a heart seeking to be free.

Beneath the arch of ancient trees,
Whispers float upon the breeze.
In shadows deep, solace blooms,
A sacred space where silence looms.

Memories carve their silent ways,
Through the dense fog and fading rays.
Each moment holds a secret dear,
In the stillness, all becomes clear.

Around the bend, the world unfurls,
Draped in the dream of hidden pearls.
Lines of solitude softly thread,
Connecting thoughts we dare not shed.

So walk these paths, embrace the night,
For in solitude, we find the light.
A fleeting breath, a gentle sigh,
In stillness, we learn to rise and fly.

A Tapestry of Frosted Dreams

On the window, frost paints fine lace,
A delicate realm, a whispered space.
Each crystal spark a story spun,
Of midnight whispers, of dreams begun.

In quiet corners, shadows play,
Dancing lightly, they drift away.
The breath of winter tells a tale,
Of wishes made on the softest gale.

Every flake, a wish set free,
In the tapestry's woven spree.
Beneath a blanket of silent white,
Magic lingers in the cold, still night.

Glimmers of hope in a shivering dawn,
Tenacious dreams, though soft and drawn.
With each sunrise, the frost will fade,
Yet the essence of dreams will never jade.

So let us weave with threads of light,
Into the fabric of yearning bright.
For every dream that takes its flight,
Is a journey born in the heart's delight.

Echoes of Chill in Forgotten Places

In shadows cast by time's embrace,
Whispers float in an empty space.
Cold winds carry tales untold,
Of lovers lost and dreams of old.

The silence hums a mournful tune,
Beneath the watchful, silver moon.
Footprints fade on paths of yore,
Each breath a memory, longing for more.

The ache of chill lingers long,
Wrapped in echoes of an ancient song.
Brick by brick, the past unveils,
In every creak, a story trails.

Through cracked walls, the wind still sighs,
Soft reverberations, where silence lies.
Forgotten corners, shrouded in mist,
Yearn for voices the world has missed.

As shadows stretch and daylight wanes,
We gather the threads of joy and pains.
In forgotten places, the heart can heal,
Embracing the chill, allowing to feel.

The Canvas of a Snowy Reverie

A blanket of white on the ground,
Whispers of dreams gently found.
Footprints in powder, they trace,
Stories of laughter, lost in space.

The trees wear a crown of pure frost,
In silence, the world seems embossed.
Breathe in the chill, let it ignite,
Magic unfolds in the soft twilight.

Each flake a tale, unique in turn,
In the calm, soft echoes we learn.
Painted in hues of silence and grace,
A moment suspended, time's embrace.

Night stretches wide, stars softly gleam,
In this canvas, we dare to dream.
The moon drapes her veil over head,
Colors of slumber, gently spread.

With every chill, the heart beats bold,
In a reverie, memories unfold.
Let the snowy embrace be our guide,
In this serene, enchanted ride.

Glacial Mirth in the Hollow Night

Under the cloak of twilight's hush,
Laughter echoes in the winter's rush.
Stars twinkle like eyes, alive and bright,
Casting glacial mirth in the hollow night.

Snowflakes spiral, a dance in the air,
Whispers of joy, gentle and rare.
In the stillness, spirits take flight,
Awash in the glow of the moon's light.

Crackling fires throw shadows long,
In the depth of night, we all belong.
Frost-kissed dreams twirl, twine, and weave,
As laughter blooms, in webs we believe.

Voices gather, like songs from afar,
Each note a promise, a shining star.
The winter's laughter, a sweet respite,
In the winged embrace of the frigid night.

Crisp air sharpens our senses anew,
In a world wrapped in silver and blue.
With hearts aglow, and spirits bright,
We revel in joy, under stars alight.

The Calm Voice of the Icebound Wind

Through the willows, the whispers glide,
A calm voice where secrets abide.
Feeling the chill brush against the skin,
The icebound wind dances within.

Each gust a tale, soft and unhurried,
In valleys deep, where echoes have flurried.
Nature's embrace, cool and serene,
Breathes life into places unseen.

Through frosted branches, a melody flows,
In tranquil moments, the spirit grows.
Haunting and sweet, it softly bends,
In the chill of night, the calm transcends.

The world hushed, as frost settles low,
Listening deep to the winds that blow.
Carrying dreams from afar they send,
Wrapping the heart in a soothing blend.

Like a whispered prayer under the stars,
The icebound wind heals all our scars.
In its embrace, we find our way,
A calm voice guiding through night and day.

In the Embrace of the Shivering Earth

Beneath the frost, the ground holds tight,
In the embrace of the shivering night.
Grass bowed low, kissed by cold,
Stories of warmth, quietly told.

The earth sighs deep, a gentle tune,
Wrapped in crystal, beneath the moon.
In the stillness, life pauses, then stirs,
As nature dons her wintry furs.

Quietly stitched, the fabric of time,
A tapestry woven, pure and sublime.
With every breath, we feel the beat,
Of the shivering earth, beneath our feet.

The stars twinkle down, a sacred light,
Illuminating paths through the cold night.
In this embrace, we seek what's near,
The touch of silence, calming our fear.

Fires may flicker, but dreams glow bright,
In the hearth of the earth, all feels right.
In winter's cradle, our spirits rise,
In the embrace of the earth, we find the skies.

Untold Stories Beneath Layers of Snow

A whisper stirs beneath the white,
Secrets hidden out of sight.
Each flake a tale long left unsaid,
In silence, dreams of poets' bread.

Footprints fade in the winter's chill,
Echoes linger on the hill.
Frozen rivers guard their lore,
Stories wait to be explored.

A world transformed to crystal sheen,
Nature dons a frosty queen.
Memory dances in the glow,
Of untold stories, none will know.

In every drift, a moment caught,
The battles fought, the love sought.
Beneath the layers, life still breathes,
Awakening as springtime weaves.

So let the snow fall ever deep,
In its embrace, we quietly keep.
The sacred past beneath the snow,
Untold tales we yearn to know.

Illumination in Hushed Absence

In quiet corners, shadows play,
Light limns the edges of the day.
Silence speaks, a gentle guide,
Through the dark, our hopes abide.

A single flame against the night,
Hushed absence transforms to light.
Each flicker dances with the air,
Whispered dreams, a tender prayer.

Where echoes linger, memories swell,
Illumined thoughts begin to tell.
In the stillness, heartbeats sound,
Beauty found in what surrounds.

The world outside may fade away,
Yet here, in grace, we choose to stay.
In luminescence soft and clear,
We find our way, we face our fear.

So let the night draw close and tight,
In hushed absence, we find our light.
Together, hand in hand we stand,
With illumination softly planned.

Nightfall Over a Frosted Landscape

As daylight wanes and shadows creep,
A frosted world prepares for sleep.
Nightfall drapes the land in blue,
Wrapped in silence, calm and true.

Stars emerge, a diamond chain,
Glittering on the frosty plain.
Moonlight bathes the world in glow,
Unlocking secrets buried low.

The crispness whispers in the air,
Nature cradles us with care.
Crickets sing a soft goodbye,
While owls hoot beneath the sky.

Each tree adorned in shimmering frost,
A beauty born from warmth now lost.
In this night, a tranquil peace,
As worries fade, and thoughts release.

Embraced by winter's cold embrace,
We find ourselves in this still place.
In nightfall's arms, our spirits play,
A frosted landscape, night will stay.

Shards of Ice in Solitary Beauty

On frozen lakes, reflections gleam,
Shards of ice, a perfect dream.
Each fragment whispers tales untold,
In icy grip, their charm behold.

Caught mid-dance, a crystal show,
Nature's art in fleeting glow.
The sun will rise, but for now,
Solitary beauty makes us vow.

Beneath the shards, a world abides,
Secrets shrouded where truth hides.
In quiet moments, we can find,
Echoes of the heart entwined.

A quiet place, a tranquil sound,
In solitude, our hopes surround.
Each glimmer draws us ever near,
To shards of ice, we hold so dear.

So let the beauty claim our gaze,
In icy realms, our heart's amaze.
For in that chill, we find our spark,
In solitary beauty, we embark.

Frosted Dreams on Still Waters

Morning light begins to gleam,
On water trapped in frosty dream.
Whispers of the night recede,
In silence, gentle thoughts take seed.

Crystal flakes of white descend,
Embrace the lake as dreams suspend.
Each ripple holds a tale untold,
As nature weaves her threads of gold.

Reflections dance in pastel hues,
Soft melodies that we can choose.
Underneath the wintry sheen,
Lies a world both calm and serene.

Branches bow with silver lace,
In this tranquil, sacred space.
A moment captured, pure and bright,
Where heart and soul take wing in flight.

Frosted dreams on water's face,
Invite us to this peaceful place.
With every breath, let worries cease,
And find within this stillness, peace.

A Solitary Journey Through the Cold

Footsteps crunch on frozen ground,
In solitude, new thoughts are found.
The world around is hushed and bare,
As twilight paints the sky with care.

Every breath comes out as mist,
In the chill, soft dreams persist.
Stars awaken in the dark,
Guiding me with twinkling spark.

Echoes of the past remain,
A whispered song, both joy and pain.
Through stillness, courage starts to rise,
A journey forged beneath the skies.

A blanket white, the silence grows,
In every moment, nature glows.
Each step taken, clearer path,
A bridge across the aftermath.

Though cold winds may bite and sting,
In solitude, my spirit sings.
A solitary journey found,
In every heartbeat, life resounds.

Reflections in the Icy Mirror

Glimmers sparkle on the ice,
A mirror formed, so clear and nice.
In its depths, my thoughts collide,
With fractured dreams that I can't hide.

Shadows dance beneath the light,
Crafting stories through the night.
I search for truths within the glow,
In this frozen world, I come to know.

Whispers of the past arise,
In the stillness of the skies.
With every glance, I see the pain,
Reflections teach us to sustain.

Time stands still upon this glass,
Moments caught, but none can last.
Yet in the beauty of this place,
I find the strength to embrace grace.

Eager hope begins to form,
Through icy winds, a quiet storm.
Reflections gather, hearts grow wise,
In such stillness, spirit flies.

Solace Among the Silent Pines

Beneath the boughs, I find my peace,
Where time slows down, and worries cease.
Whispers soft as gentle sighs,
Invite the heart to clear the skies.

Shadows fall, the forest glows,
In every branch, a story flows.
Amongst the trunks both tall and grand,
I walk the path, the earth my hand.

Each needle kissed by morning dew,
A sacred space where dreams come true.
In silence deep, the spirit wakes,
And understands the choice it makes.

With every breath, the woodlands share,
A sense of hope, beyond compare.
Among the pines, I claim my space,
A refuge found, a warm embrace.

Solace wraps me, gentle and kind,
In nature's arms, the soul aligned.
Here in the still, where shadows play,
I find my heart, and here I stay.